ALLEN PHOTOGRA

HOW TO
BECOME A JUDGE

CONTENTS

INTRODUCTION

If you were to look at a judges' panel from the 1960s, you would probably find that many of the judges were titled people, ex-military or even members of the clergy. In recent years, however, showing societies have made a great effort to shed their 'closed shop' image and are now openly encouraging new and younger people to come forward for consideration as judges.

This comes at a time when there seems to be a greater interest than ever before in judges' decisions and in all judging methods. A prime example of this is the way a show secretary's office soon fills up with interested spectators and exhibitors once marking sheets are pinned up for public scrutiny after the classes have been judged.

Shows are demanding more judges each year as new competitions are introduced and restrictions on the judging of certain qualifying rounds are imposed. The relevant societies' attempts to supply this demand by appointing more judges has also given both show secretaries and competitors more choice which can only be good for showing.

LOOKING TO THE FUTURE

THE BRITISH SHOW PONY SOCIETY

NEEDS YOU

IF YOU ARE INTERESTED IN BECOMING A BSPS JUDGE, YOU ARE INVITED TO APPLY FOR PLACES ON THE 2006 TRAINING & ASSESSMENT DAYS DETAILS ATTACHED

Good judging is based on personal opinion backed up by a sound knowledge of certain values which are applicable to each class. Some judges will be influenced by the overall picture and presentation or by an exceptional ride. Others will attach more importance to correctness of conformation over performance. Each new judge should bring a fresh out-look to the showing circuit and this is what allows show-ing to evolve and makes the show ring a place of great speculation and interest.

TRAINING

If you are interested in becoming a judge, your chance of reaching the first rung of the official ladder will be seriously enhanced by your own experience in the ring, although not solely as a competitor.

Anybody can pick a winner from the ringside but not everyone can place a class from the judge's perspective. Having some experience 'behind the camera', that is, from the middle of the ring where it matters, will therefore be an advantage when applying to become a judge. In fact, some organisations insist on this criterion.

Stewarding can provide valuable experience as it not only allows you to study a class from a great vantage point, but you may also pick up useful tips while standing alongside a knowledgeable judge, as well as becoming increasingly familiar with routine procedures such as awarding special rosettes and qualification cards.

Once confident in the role of steward, a natural progression would be to try your hand at judging at some smaller, unaffiliated shows. There is no better grounding than hands-on experience.

Attending seminars and breed society study days will give you the opportunity of listening to an exchange of ideas which may not only prove thought provoking but should increase your knowledge of what to look out for. 'Fun' judging contests and young judges' competitions can also be enjoyable and will give you a chance to voice your opinions – all good practice for assessment days.

YOUNG JUDGES' COMPETITIONS

With an eye on the future, many societies are now encouraging their younger members to participate in various young judges' competitions and training schemes. The most successful of these is the British Show Pony Society (BSPS) Young Judges' Competition, held on the East of England Showground just before the society's national championship show.

Each geographical BSPS area (of which there are 24, plus Scotland and Ireland) nominates a team comprising three members between the ages of 14 to 21 years old, plus an individual between the ages of 18 and 24 years old.

The team members will be expected to work as a group, whereas the individual competitor will undergo a one-to-one assessment with a senior judge.

Prior to the competition, potential candidates will receive the benefit of invaluable training and tuition provided by their area, giving them an opportunity to expand their knowledge of the judging process.

Method of Judging

The competition is judged as a ridden showing class using a marking system. After judging, candidates will be required to answer questions on the placing of the ponies, their way of going and conformation and on the rules and regulations that apply.

ASSESSMENT DAYS

With some sound, relevant experience under your belt, as soon as you feel ready for the next stage you must decide where your interests lie and which type of horses/ponies you would like to judge. Our advice is to take one step at a time and not apply for several panels all at once, especially as some rules may vary from society to society, which can be confusing.

Different showing societies may have slightly different application procedures but normally this involves supplying a *curriculum vitae* (CV), together with a fee, and completing a questionnaire about your experience. However, some bodies also insist on a reference from an existing judge and/or a member of that particular organisation. There might be an upper and lower age limit for candidates. You may also have to become a member of the relevant society before applying. For example, the Welsh Pony &

APPLICATION FORM FOR ASSESSMENT DAY 2006

I wish to take part in the Assessment Day for Future Judges to be held at
Endon Riding School, Stanley Moss Lane, Stoke on Trent, Staffs.

ENTRY FEE: £50 (Cheques payable to BSPS)
Judges already on a BSPS Panel £25

Both sides of this application form MUST be completed.

NAME_____

ADDRESS_____

_____TEL:_____

BSPS MEMBERSHIP NO:_____

AGE if under 25years:-_____

Which Panel do you wish to be assessed for? - (Please tick)

SHOW PONY_____   SHOW HUNTER PONY_____

WORKING HUNTER PONY_____

HERITAGE PANEL_____

Please Note Candidates may only be assessed for **ONE** panel.

I confirm that I have read and agree to abide by the BSPS Constitution and Rules and Regulations and I agree to abide by the Assessors and the Assessment Committee's decisions:-

SIGNED_____

*The reverse side of this form is shown on the following page.

Cob Society will only consider applications from candidates who have been members for at least seven consecutive years, thereby demonstrating both loyalty and an understanding of the breed. At the time of writing, before applying for the National Pony Society Mountain & Moorland panel, a candidate is required to have been on an individual breed panel for several years.

Some organisations run 'mock' assessment/ training days before the big day itself, which give candidates a helpful insight into the format. These can provide a valuable,

1) What experience have you had with ponies ?_____
_____
_____

2) What experience have you had with horses?_____
_____
_____

3) Riding experience ?_____
_____
_____
_____

4) Showing experience ?_____
_____
_____
_____
_____

5) Are you on any other Judges Panel?_____
_____

6) Have you had any experience Judging ?
(a) Affiliated Shows_____
(b) Unaffiliated Shows_____

7) Have you attended a Training Day, Teach In or Conference ?_____
If yes give details _____

8) Have you had any experience Stewarding?_____

9) Have you had any experience Marking BSPS classes?_____

confidence-boosting rehearsal so that the actual assessment days do not appear too daunting.

BSPS ASSESSMENT DAYS

At the BSPS Assessment Day candidates are expected to judge a class as normal, using the marking system. Working Hunter Pony candidates are also expected to walk the course beforehand and to spot any deliberate mistakes. Candidates will be interviewed later about their findings and placings. There is also a separate interview on BSPS rules and regulations. Candidates are recalled later in the day to be told if they have passed or failed, which is considered by many to be a better system than waiting for a letter to arrive weeks later in the post.

If not successful, the candidate will normally be told why and will usually be encouraged to have another go the following year. Some of today's leading judges were unsuccessful on their first attempt, so our advice is to keep trying, just as you would with a motor car driving test!

The BSPS has an interesting system whereby a high-calibre candidate may be fast-tracked straight onto the panel in the following year. If borderline, however, a candidate might be expected to probation at a maximum number of shows.

RIDE PANELS

At the British Show Hack Cob & Riding Horse Association (BSHC&RHA) assessment, candidates who are applying for the ride panel will be expected to ride competently and possess the ability to compare and assess the rides, as well as to discuss their findings with the appointed senior assessors.

Candidates will also study the conformation of individual horses and answer questions posed by each assessor assigned to that horse. It is essential to have a good knowledge of conformation faults and horse and pony types: you might even be asked whether the animal in front of you is a show horse and, if so, which class it should go in.

Interviews are also prominent on this association's agenda and candidates will be asked questions about their experience, availability to judge, rules and regulations and how they would handle different judging scenarios.

THE ARAB HORSE SOCIETY

Potential judges for the Arab Horse Society will be expected to attend a number of training, educational and examination courses before taking part in probationary judging. Successful candidates are then invited to attend a final assessment which will include a written test on rules, conformation, type, faults and defects, ringcraft and judging methods.

THE IMPORTANCE OF CONFORMATION

A horse with correct conformation will not only be pleasing to the eye, but should, in theory, remain sounder and be more comfortable to ride than a horse with poor conformation. A serious conformation fault will put more strain on the horse's joints and structure. A horse may be ill mannered in the show ring on one day only, whereas a horse with bad conformation will have bad conformation throughout its entire life.

SOME OF THE ELEMENTS THAT CONSTITUTE 'A GOOD RIDE':

- Balance, lightness and suppleness

- Comfort

- Obedience

- Education

- Between hand and leg

- Good stride

- Going in a straight line

- Correct bend

- Waiting for the rider's commands and not anticipating

AUTHORS' TIPS

- Candidates must show an ability to cope with the pressures of modern-day judging. As with any examination procedure, it is important to remain focused and not let your nerves get the better of you.

- Take a clipboard, paper and pen if you envisage writing notes. (For example, this will be expected at the BSPS assessment day.)

- Make sure you can see the animals clearly as they walk away and trot towards you in a straight line, especially when you are part of a group.

Authors' Tips continue on next page

- If applying for a ride panel, it is imperative that candidates are riding fit and have a wide experience of riding unfamiliar horses.

- Dress should be smart, practical and correct.

- Make sure you are fully conversant with rules and procedures. If you cannot remember the answer to a rule question, say that, as a judge, you would always have a rule book with you for reference.

- Use the correct terminology (for examplo, windgalls rather than 'puffy ankles') and familiar phrases (for example:
  'This pony lacks scope.';
  'This pony has a good top line.';
  'This horse lacks bone.';
  'This horse is back at the knee.').

- Be clear and precise during the interview.

- Use the marking system correctly, making sure you can back up your decisions with sound reasoning in your interview.

ASSESSING CONFORMATION

Employ a consistent method when assessing conformation. Whether this involves examining the animal from head to toe or from the feet upwards, it must, however, include the whole picture. With this in mind you can see whether the animal is well proportioned (for example, not higher behind than in front or overtopped for its limbs) and we often find that standing back to obtain a general view is the best place to start. Remember to look at both sides as well as from in front and behind the horse. Your job will be made easier if the horse is standing correctly.

TYPICAL QUESTIONS AND POSSIBLE ANSWERS

During the interview you may be asked questions about common judging situations.

Q How would you deal with an irate exhibitor?

A Be polite and avoid getting into an unpleasant argument. Be brief with your explanation, adding that it is your opinion on the day. Don't be aloof or appear rude by totally ignoring the situation.

Q How would you keep to the timetable?

A If there is a large number of entries and you are struggling with time, discuss this with your steward as he or she can help you enormously. Don't ride the horses for longer than is necessary. Bring the horses back to the line up rather than finishing the ride in a remote corner and wasting valuable time walking the horse back into line. Have your steward make sure the stirrup leathers are the correct length for you and that the next horse is available to ride immediately you dismount from the previous one. If time will not allow you to ride each exhibit, that's your call. If required, have exhibitors do a short, set show rather than a freestyle one, possibly two at a time. Have the next horse/pony out ready for conformation while assessing the previous one. Pull horses forward into a final order rather than walk them round. Have rosettes ready for presentation.

Q When does a class finish?

A The class finishes when the judge instructs the steward to move the class off after rosette presentation. If horses misbehave before then, even during rosette presentation, the judge is at liberty to change the order. However, you would not retrieve the class if an animal behaves badly on the lap of honour.

Q What happens if a steward warns you about an animal being naughty behind you?

A Even though you have been made aware of the fact, you cannot act on it as you have not seen it yourself.

Q What do you think makes a good judge?

A A good judge must be aware of correct type, conformation, soundness, performance, what constitutes a good ride and the rules appertaining to that class and must undertake the task in a courteous manner, particularly when dealing with children. A sign of a good judge is when exhibitors have been able to follow the placings and the judge has handled situations such as misbehaviour consistently.

PROBATIONARY JUDGING

Use this opportunity to pick up as much experience as possible. Your senior judge will not be expecting you to know everything and neither will you be expected to agree totally with the senior judge. However, you will be encouraged to commit yourself to firm and speedy decisions even though these will not influence the final outcome.

Certain conditions and regulations may apply regarding probationary judging, so check with the person in charge of the judging scheme. For instance, you may have to probation outside of your own home area and not be able to probation with your referee sponsors, assessors or friends. In some instances you will not be able to exhibit at the show on the same day that you fulfil your probationary duties.

DOS AND DON'TS

As soon as you have been appointed to the probationary panel, waste no time in arranging your shows. Those who leave it to the last minute often have to travel further afield which is an important consideration because you will bear these expenses yourself. Make contact with both the show secretary and the senior judge with whom you wish to serve your probation and make sure all arrangements are understood on all sides. If an emergency occurs and you are unable to keep an appointment, again make sure all other parties are informed.

Be punctual and arrive at a show in plenty of time. Introduce yourself to the secretary and judge on arrival. Be aware that sometimes there may be a build up of traffic entering the showground,

which can cause delays. Arriving late would create a bad impression. Dress must be practical and smart and you should display any probationary badges/armbands as applicable so that exhibitors clearly understand your role.

Keep close to your senior judge without getting in the way or obstructing his or her view and become sufficiently involved in the judging process so that the senior judge can assess your ability to place the horses/ponies in front of you. Be alert as you will be expected to act quickly if unexpected situations arise.

Be confident without being familiar, whether dealing with the judge or sponsors, exhibitors or stewards, both inside and outside the ring.

Keep comments quiet and never discuss your findings with anyone after the class, even if approached. You must declare an interest if you have had any relevant dealings with an animal or exhibitor in the ring and then you will probably be precluded from judging it. After the judging, hand over any relevant paperwork to the senior judge.

THE BRITISH SHOW HACK, COB & RIDING HORSE ASSOCIATION

2 High Street, Hitchin, SG5 1BH
Tel: 01462 437770 Fax: 01462 437776
Website: showhackandcob.org.uk
Email: admin@showhackandcob.org.uk

PROBATIONARY JUDGES REPORT - 2006
CONFIDENTIAL TO THE COMMITTEE

Probationer:..

Show ....

Date: ....

Class: ....

Number of Exhibits in class:..

Name of Judge: ....

Turnout: .... **Punctuality**:...........................
....

Manner:.. **Riding Ability & Fitness**...............
....

Knowledge of Conformation................. **Knowledge of Type**:.......................
....

**Could he/she conduct and control
a large class efficiently**....................... ....
....
....

Any other comments............................
....
....
.... **Judges Signature**
....
.... Please return this completed form to the
                                                   Secretary: Mrs T Monaghan Hulatt, 2 High Street,
                                                   Herts, SG5 1BH.

JUDGING ETIQUETTE

As an ambassador of the showing world and the showing body you are representing, you should be polite, act with integrity and dignity and treat the judging appointment as an honour. Always remember that exhibitors have paid money for your honest opinion and that the value of the stock in front of you could increase or decrease following your placings.

Judging is about comparing like with like, assessing all the good points and faults to enable you to end up with that all important result. You must judge a class with a completely open mind and judge what you see in front of you on the day. Unlike racing and show-jumping where the winner is obvious to all, showing is subjective (just like the appreciation of art or music) and the results are based on your own personal opinion. If an outstanding horse that you have judged before has not gone well enough to stand top on this particular occasion, then so be it. In today's showing world your actions have to be accountable.

The relationship with your steward is all important as he or she is there to assist you in the smooth running of the classes and should also keep you up to date with the time. As with exhibitors, do not be overly chatty with the stewards even if you know them personally. It is important not only to be impartial but to be seen to be impartial. If you are being distracted by a very talkative steward or he is blocking your view, politely ask him to modify his behaviour. Be aware of making in-depth comments to exhibitors, especially children, as these can sometimes be misconstrued.

Co-judging can be fun and should not be thought of as a battle of wits as you are both on the same side. On occasion, it may be necessary to reach a compromise to obtain a satisfactory result if you fail to agree, but try to avoid

> **AUTHORS' TIP**
> When ride judging do not abuse your position by riding any horse for longer than usual, even though you may be having an enjoyable time!

requesting a referee as one may not be available. Some societies allow the conformation judge to be the more senior judge with the final say in a contentious decision. When judging in a group in a supreme championship, approach the task with an open mind as your champion may not be the best overall on the day.

Do not take on too many appointments of a similar kind, especially in the same area in one season. Never let an event down even if a more prestigious show invites you to judge for them instead on the same day.

INTERNATIONAL JUDGING

On occasion, judges are privileged to be invited to judge abroad. A good judge will adapt well to these situations, even when the judging procedures or marking systems are different to those in the UK. The principles are the same even if the criteria are unfamiliar.

IN THE RING

- When entering the ring make sure the area is safe and the entry points and exits are clearly controlled. Assess the best places to ride the animals, line them up, change the rein, perform individual shows and stand each horse up for conformation judging, avoiding obstacles such as show jumps and bad ground.

- Try to watch one side of the ring for the majority of the time on the go round. If you keep turning round to observe just a few competitors, you are likely to miss some of the others. Try to avoid watching the class riding downhill.

- Keep focused and always acknowledge the end of an individual show. It is when a judge loses concentration, even for a split second, that animals inevitably misbehave or something happens out of the blue, often making it difficult to assess the true situation.

- Do not ask the breeding of animals until after a championship.

- Try not to handle the animals when judging. However, if you feel it is essential to run a hand down a horse's leg to clarify a point, do this to some other horses as well and then you will not send messages out to the ring-side that you might have found something detrimental in respect of one particular animal.

- Judges have been instructed to look unfavourably on overly fat animals, particularly youngstock.

- Use the full range of marks in order to obtain an accurate result, make sure your steward writes them down correctly and check them before rosette presentation.

- After the initial go round, be ready to pull the animals in swiftly. There is nothing worse than when a class has been going round for 15 minutes and the judge only pulls in a couple of competitors before sending them off again at trot; or when judges keep horses on a final walk round for an eternity or, worse still, when those at the end of the line up are not called in and are still walking around while the judge is presenting the rosettes. You should never ignore those at the end of the line as they have paid the same entry money.

- When judging on a triangle, (usually sport horse/pony breeding classes) make sure you are in a position to see the animals perform coming towards and going away from you, as well as in profile.

UNSOUNDNESS

If, in your opinion, an animal is unsound, you should give the exhibitor the option of being placed at the bottom of the line or withdrawing from the class. If a vet's opinion is sought and no vet is available, the judge's decision is final.

THE DEBATE ON MANNERS

Whereas some judges will not accept anything other than a flawless performance, others do not see the situation that simply. 'We are judging show animals,' they say, 'not police horses, and part of the make up of a top show animal is for it to have *joie de vivre*.'

Obviously, children on small ponies must feel secure and ponies should be 'patent safety', but does this apply to bigger animals? If an older rider is not in danger, should a bigger pony/horse be penalised in the same way? If an animal goes on the wrong leg for a split second, say, a novice pony due to a momentary lapse of concentration, but is outstanding in the class, should it be penalised to the same degree as an animal that continues on the wrong leg for half its show or has a wrong strike off due to an incorrect way of going?

CONCLUSION

Whether judging in hand or ridden sections, jumping or flat classes, the duties of the modern-day judge have changed slightly. Good knowledge of horseflesh is as essential as ever, but these days the judge must also be aware of health and safety issues, comply with the ever-increasing rules and requirements of the class (including awarding special rosettes) and possess good people skills as well as being literate and numerate. If you ever have to comment on your judging via a microphone or to the press, remember to be diplomatic. Don't tell the world what was wrong with the top horse that you put down the line. Instead, be informative in general terms or give positive reasons why you made a particular horse champion on the day.

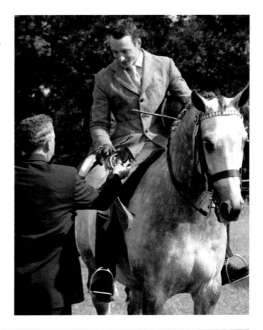

Judging is an ever-changing process and judges are expected to attend conferences/workshops if they are to keep up with growing trends, new rules and the latest problems. These events can work beneficially in both directions, however, as judges then also have an opportunity to express their concerns and discuss improvements with the relevant ruling body. One must never stop adding to one's knowledge, even as a fully fledged judge.

OUR FINAL WORD

Enjoy your judging at whatever level you are at as each appointment should be seen as a completely unique and challenging experience. It is often said that there are only two people who are happy after a class – the judge and the winner. However, this is not always true as the judge's favourite may have had an off day and be standing down the line. Remember, you cannot please everybody and the decision based on the judge's opinion on the day is final.

Dedicated to our father, George Hollings

ACKNOWLEDGEMENTS

The authors wish to express their gratitude to Gill Genders for kindly sponsoring this book.

Our thanks must also go to the following photographers:

Penelope Barlow – www.penelopebarlow.co.uk   Sally Coles – s.colesphoto@btopenworld.com
Gill & Chris Cook – info@pleaseureprints.co.uk   Steve Dawe (Real Time Imaging) –
www.rtiphotography.co.uk   Ken Ettridge – www.kenettphoto.co.uk .

A special thank you also to *Horse & Hound* and the picture editor
Alex Medhurst for their contribution.

Other books in the series written by the Hollings brothers include:

No 6 Producing Ridden Show Ponies, Nigel Hollings
No 7 Showing In Hand, Stuart Hollings
No 14 Ringcraft, Stuart and Nigel Hollings

British Library Cataloguing-in-Publication Data
A catalogue record for this book is available from the British Library

ISBN 978-0-85131-925-4

Published in Great Britain in 2007
by J.A. Allen
Clerkenwell House, 45–47 Clerkenwell Green,
London EC1R OHT

J.A. Allen is an imprint of Robert Hale Limited

Design and Typesetting by Paul Saunders
Edited by Lesley Young
Colour separation by Tenon & Polert Colour Scanning Limited, Hong Kong
Printed by Gutenberg Press Limited, Malta